The
IMAGINE IT
BOOK

Discover, Create, and Invent
Our Amazing Future!

by **Ellen Sabin**

and _____

WRITE YOUR NAME HERE

WATERING CAN® PRESS

www.wateringcanpress.com

WATERING CAN®

Growing Kids with Character

When you care about things and nurture them,
they will grow healthy, strong, and happy, and in turn,
they will make the world a better place.

All Watering Can Press titles are available at special quantity discounts for bulk purchases
for sales promotion, premiums, fund-raising, educational, or institutional use.

Watering Can Press offers customized versions of this book and will adjust content for use
by nonprofits and corporations in support of their community outreach and marketing goals.

**To inquire about bulk discounts or to learn more about customized book runs,
please visit our website or e-mail info@wateringcanpress.com.**

Text and illustrations © 2017 by Ellen Sabin

WATERING CAN is a registered trademark of Ellen Sabin.

Written by Ellen Sabin
Illustrated by Kerren Barbas
Designed by Elynn Cohen
Art p. 31 by Bob Englehart

ISBN: 978-0-9826416-1-3
Printed in China in August 2017

Website address: www.wateringcanpress.com

Dear _____ ,

Because you have a huge imagination, I am giving you **THE IMAGINE IT BOOK**.

As you use it, you will realize that when you pay attention to the ideas in your imagination, you have the power to turn them into inventions and discoveries.

You will learn how these new things can bring health, safety, entertainment, and happiness to people and make the world a better place.

Along the way, you'll get to play, think, build, and learn as you write your own book and fill it with your thoughts, ideas, drawings, and inspirations.

I hope this book will help you plan your steps to creating a future filled with your amazing ideas.

From, _____

Some "thank-yous"

- To my mom—my best editor and critic, and an inspiration for following my own ideas and inventing a future of my creation.

- Thank you to Craig Allen, Martin Fisher, Sonal Shaw, and Tom Gruber for sprinkling their bits of genius, creativity, and passion for innovation in my mind and on these pages.

- There were many professionals—inventors, innovators, educators, and thinkers—who contributed their time, expertise, encouragement, and support. I especially want to thank Hope Chafiian, Joshua Schuler, and Alexé Weymouth.

A NOTE TO ADULTS

Imagination is magical. How amazing would our world be if children maintained the joy and wonder that imagination brings?

The IMAGINE IT BOOK is meant to inspire children to nurture their ideas and encourage them to harness their creative power to become lifelong learners, thinkers, and problem-solvers.

Through using this book, children will connect science, technology, engineering, and math (STEM) topics to the real world and find opportunities to shape the future through invention and discovery.

Along the way, this book will engage children in questioning, collaborating, taking risks, problem solving, logical thinking, and hands-on activities that will build their confidence and their character.

Ultimately, I hope The IMAGINE IT BOOK journey will inspire children toward a lifetime habit of following their ideas with joy and purpose as they make a difference in the world and solve tomorrow's problems.

Table of Contents

What is The
IMAGINE IT BOOK?

Imagination is the fun, amazing, exciting process of creating new ideas.

Ideas let you picture things not just as they are, but as they could be.

When you make up a story in your head, you can see it, hear it, and even smell it. You can create a new way to travel in your head—like a machine that lets you jump over buildings. You can imagine a new way to help the planet by collecting energy from mud, plants, or even stars. You can think up a new potion that gives you a superpower; a device that lets you read other people's minds; or a way to talk to animals so you could ask your dog or cat how it's feeling today.

YOU use your imagination all the time.

Every time you let your mind wander and pretend, you are using your imagination. Every time you daydream about faraway places or exotic creatures, you are using your imagination. Sometimes you use your imagination when you aren't even trying—like when you're reading a book, listening to a story, or even asleep and dreaming.

When you have a new idea, you can nurture it.
You can give it attention, care for it, work with it, and play with it!
When you do this, anything becomes possible.

★ You will find that your idea becomes magical.
★ It will want to be shared.
★ It will become better than you ever thought possible.
★ It will make you feel good.
★ It will get bigger and bigger.

When you nurture the ideas from your imagination, you have the power to make them into real-life discoveries and inventions.
YOU can create a future full of your ideas!

What are you waiting for? Turn the page and get started! • • • ➤

People use their imaginations to invent and discover new things.

An **invention** is a new thing or a new way of doing something. Some inventions are useful and practical (like a fork) and others (like the Internet) are giant and world changing.

An **innovation** is something created to improve on a past invention, making it different, better, or more useful. Inventions and innovations are usually created to improve life by filling a need or solving a problem.

A **discovery** is something that already exists but only becomes known about when someone sees it for the first time—like a new place, animal, or plant. When someone understands something for the first time, that's also a discovery. For example, it was a discovery when scientists figured out that gravity is why people stay grounded on Earth instead of floating away into outer space. People always want to know more about the world.

Why do people invent and discover?

It usually starts with an idea that they can't stop thinking about. They want to explore and nurture their idea. And when they do, it can lead to inventions and discoveries that:

- ★ save lives
- ★ help people
- ★ make life easier
- ★ entertain people

- ★ create new businesses
- ★ protect animals or the planet
- ★ connect people with one another

Who are the people who invent, innovate, and discover?

They are people who use their imaginations and let their minds play. Some want to know more about how the world works, and others want to figure out ways to solve problems to make the world better.

They are people just like YOU!

Now that you know where your imagination can take you, you can jump in and start your journey to discover, create, and invent with THE IMAGINE IT BOOK!

First You get to learn and think about some amazing inventions and discoveries.

Next You think about the qualities of people who create new things—how they act and what they do to turn their ideas into reality.

Then You IMAGINE even more. You can think about what YOU want to create, discover, and invent.

And You get to DO THINGS—take steps and make plans—to share your ideas and creations with the world.

Then You get to imagine, create, discover, and invent OVER and OVER and OVER again as you have fun and fill the world with your ideas!

REMEMBER: This is YOUR book. Along the way, you can fill in the blanks, draw pictures, and collect ideas about all the great things you can do with your amazing imagination.

Celebrating Discoveries and Inventions!

Inventions and discoveries often have one big thing in common: They began with someone thinking, **"What if . . ."**

What if we could fly? Airplanes

What if we were outside and wanted to see in the dark? Flashlights and Batteries

What if we found a way to reduce the amount of trash in the world? Recycling

What if there were a way to keep people from getting a disease? Vaccines

What if people wanted to keep track of time? Clocks

Discoveries and Inventions Are Everywhere

Every hour of every single day, you are using or seeing something that someone invented or discovered.

Internet • car • jeans • wheel • pencil • X-rays • skateboard • chair • soccer ball • camera • rockets • cell phone • mirror • stethoscope • plastic • glasses • dinosaurs • Pluto • video game • cheese • money • tunnel • magnets • roads • chocolate • radio • antibiotics • GPS • refrigerator • gold • sail boat • steam engine • hammer • drone • kevlar • fire • battery • paper • laser • DNA • electricity • ice cream cone • eraser • submarine • steel • map • television • nail polish • computer • telescope • glass • washing machine • hearing aid • frisbee • soap • movies • crayon • battery • braille • sunscreen • oxygen • fingerprints • puzzle • hanger • spoon • ruler • skyscraper • watch • pizza • cement • penicillin • calendar • bicycle • snowboard • photosynthesis • air conditioner • abacus 3-D printing • film • microscope • candle • plough • chess staircase • gravity • oven • plastic • language • shoelaces

There's not enough room on this page, or in this book, or in 100 books to list them all.

And new discoveries and inventions are being added all the time.

What Is the Problem or Need?

Inventions are usually created to help get stuff
done or make things better.

Match the problems listed below with the inventions that helped solve them.

This food is cold.

My pants are too big. I need something so they don't fall down.

I need these papers to stay together.

I need to find some information.

fire   belt   zipper

library   stapler

STOVE

button   notebook   paperclip

microwave   Internet

books

safety pin   newpaper

The History of Communication

Long ago, stories were passed down over generations to keep the tales alive. Over time, many inventions were created to help people connect, communicate, and spread ideas.

Ideas were first recorded by carving pictures into stone. Later, people made up alphabets and formed them into words.

People discovered a way to record words on scrolls, which allowed ideas to spread more easily. After that, books were written on animal skin and later, when it was invented, on paper. At first, books were written by hand, so it took a really long time to make a single book.

People also wanted to communicate directly with others, so they wrote letters and invented mail systems to send personal messages.

The printing press was invented so books could be produced easier and faster. That meant more people could have books.

The telegraph was invented to send messages faster. Then the telephone made connecting even easier. It was a big deal because it let people hear one another from far away.

Mobile phones were invented so people no longer needed to be in a building with a landline to connect—they could be anywhere!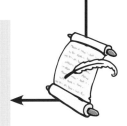

There have been many other inventions throughout history that have connected people. Here are just a few more: smoke signals, typewriters, newspapers, radio, TV, sign language, two-way radio, the Internet, e-mail, and virtual reality.

People never stop trying to improve on past inventions to make new ones that are even safer, easier, faster, or better in other ways.

Have You Ever Wondered

Why twins look alike?   How our brains remember things?

How a compass works?   How mirrors work?

How people build tunnels under water without water getting inside them?

How bears know when to hibernate?

If prosthetic arms feel what they touch?

How video chatting works?

How the ancient pyramids were built without modern tools and machines?

Why two guitars sound different from each other?

How a thermos keeps hot things hot and cold things cold?

Why long bridges don't sag in the middle?

What's the best material to use to build a bike that is super lightweight?

Why people don't fall out of roller coasters that go upside down?

Why planets move the way they do?

These are all examples of questions that science, technology, engineering, and math can answer.

It's pretty cool—questions are unanswered until someone figures out a way to answer them.

If you ask an adult for help, you can find the answers to all these questions. That's because someone already spent time solving these mysteries.

Imagine being the first
person to answer a BIG question!

Living in New Places

People have always created places to live to keep their families safe and comfortable. We have invented houses, apartment buildings, houseboats, RVs, and more.

Everyone lives and shares space on our planet, and over time, it's getting more crowded. To help solve that problem, some people are thinking about inventing ways to live in new places—like on the water, under water, or in outer space.

Use your imagination and pretend you are living in one of these new places. Or create another place in your mind. Write a story about your visit to this place.

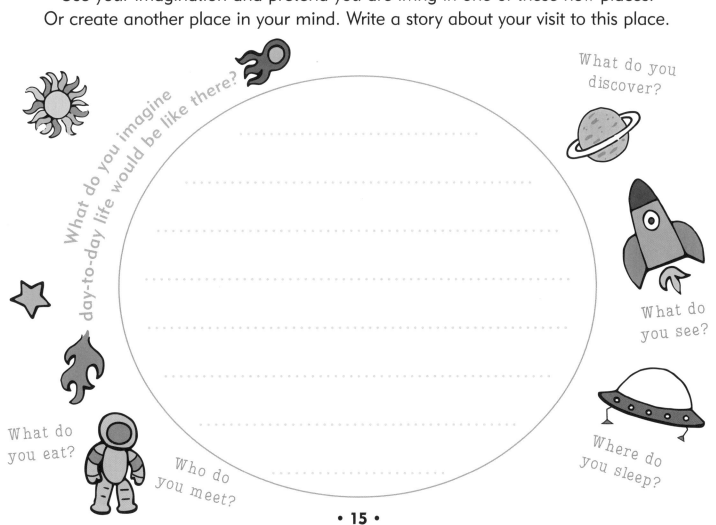

What do you imagine day-to-day life would be like there?

What do you discover?

What do you see?

Where do you sleep?

What do you eat?

Who do you meet?

An Invention Hunt

You've probably heard of a scavenger hunt, right? In this version of the game, you get to search for inventions. They're everywhere!

Start at your front door and walk through your house to your bedroom.

Write down ten objects that you notice along the way.

Guess what? Everything you wrote down was invented by someone!

For example, if you saw a chair, someone (or perhaps a team of people) had to invent, design, and build it. Maybe you saw a light switch. Someone discovered electricity, and that switch was invented to turn the power on and off. Did you look out a window? Someone discovered how to make glass, and then someone else invented the window.

Invention Investigation

Now, take one of the items you found, or pick something else you use every day. It can be anything. It can be something silly or useful, big or small, invented recently or long ago.

It's time to do some research and learn about your object.

Why do you think this item was invented? (What problem did it solve or need did it fill?) ....

What materials were used to make it? Why do you think those materials were chosen? ....

....

Some items can be traced back to the person who first invented them. Others were developed by many people working together. If your item can be traced back, who invented it? When?

....

Now use your imagination. If you were going to improve on this item, what would you do to make it better?
Hint: Think about ways it could be easier to use, look or feel better, or have other things added or changed to make it even more useful.

....

....

....

Gifts Discovered from the Earth

People use gifts from the earth—or our natural resources—to make our lives better. Over the years, inventors and scientists have found ways to use materials and resources from our planet (like diamonds, gold, coal, lead, and water) to create pencils, tools, jewelry, circuit boards, and many other things you use every day.

Some of the useful gifts our planet has given to us are called "fossil fuels." Fossil fuels were created from material (called peat) that was buried underground millions of years ago.

Gas, oil, and coal are all fossil fuels.

Each of these fuels is used to create energy. Sometimes this energy is used to make electricity, power cars, heat homes, or run many of the machines and appliances we use every day.

A lot of our electricity gets its energy from fossil fuels. But there are other ways to make electricity, too. Electricity and energy can also be made by using the power of the wind, water, or sun.

Below, make a list of things you like using every day that need electricity to work.

....

....

....

....

Wow! Now you can say a special "thank-you" to the inventors and scientists whose ideas and efforts created energy sources that make your favorite things work.

The Inventor Hall of Fame

There are many people who have made a difference in the world by inventing things.

Do some research about the invention heroes listed below. You can use the Internet or the library, or you can ask a parent or teacher. Then decide who your favorite is and why.

Marie Curie
What did she do?

....

....

Leonardo da Vinci
What did he do?

....

....

George Washington Carver
What did he do?

....

....

Ben Franklin
What did he do?

....

....

Here are some other great inventors from history:

Rachel Carson, Albert Einstein, and Maria Telkes.

There are also lots of people living today who are invention heroes!
Can you think of some?

Real People Doing Really Cool Things

"I enjoy coding. I also love playing in pretend worlds, and I get to bring those worlds to life in video games that I create."

I'm a game designer

"I study and spend time with dolphins. They have their own language, and I want to understand what they are saying."

I'm a behavioral marine biologist

"I study the human brain so I can use what I learn to make computers that 'think'."

I'm an artificial intelligence (AI) engineer

"In some parts of the world, children go blind because certain vitamins are missing from their diets. We invented a way to add vitamin A to the rice they plant so people can grow and eat rice that will keep children's eyes healthy."

I'm a genetic scientist

"I work to improve the design of the fastest train ever. This train floats in the air using magnets."

I'm a mechanical engineer

"Sometimes people get sick from infections spread through water, air, or food. My job is to try to trace the paths of infections. I use maps, science, math, and plain, old detective work to keep germs from spreading and prevent illness."

I'm an epidemiologist

"I used to dream about traveling and seeing different places and people. Now I'm creating 3-D virtual tours of communities around the world."

I'm a software developer

"I design machines that let people recover the use of limbs they have lost."

I'm a robotic prosthetic designer

"I never realized how many different things went into making an animated movie. I work with artists, software programmers, writers, and actors to make animated characters come to life."

I'm an animated film director

"I study rocks to learn more about the processes that shaped our earth. We hope this information can be used to understand earthquakes better so we can prevent and predict them more accurately."

I'm a geologist

"I love design, and I also care about our planet. I create homes that can generate nearly as much energy as they use."

I'm an energy-management architect

What Are the QUALITIES of People Who Discover and Invent?

The people who create, innovate, and discover amazing things come in all different shapes and sizes.

❁ Some are scientists, engineers, mathematicians, or people with other training and education that help them work to solve a problem or a mystery. Others are everyday people who never planned to be inventors but they create new things because they see problems that they want to solve.

❁ Some work in jobs that let them focus on discovery all day, and others create new things as a hobby or just for fun.

❁ Some are interested in many different topics and invent lots of different things, while others focus on one subject.

❁ Some hope their efforts will help people and the planet, and others hope to create businesses that make money, create jobs, or produce things for people to enjoy.

❁ These people are women and men. They may be old or very young. They are from big cities in the United States, small villages in Africa, and everywhere in between.

So you see...no matter who they are or where they come from, anyone can achieve great things, and everyone has the chance to be an inventor or creator.

BUT, there are some key qualities shared by these people.

These traits help them use their imagination
⇩
to create ideas
⇩
and then take actions
⇩
that lead to new inventions and discoveries
⇩
that can help people to be safe, healthy, informed, connected, entertained, or happy.

Observant

When someone is observant, it means that they are good at watching and listening, seeing details, and noticing what is going on around them.

Once, an observant woman named Mary Anderson noticed that drivers were wiping their car windows with their hands when it rained or snowed because they couldn't see. They had to stop, get out of their cars, get wet and cold while wiping the windows, and then drive until they had to do it all over again. She thought that there must be a better way to clean a windshield. She went on to invent and design the windshield wiper!

One way to be observant is to look around at nature, which can provide a lot of really great ideas for new inventions. For example, an inventor named George de Mestral got the idea for creating Velcro when he noticed burdock burrs (the outside of certain seeds) sticking to his pants after taking a walk. He looked closely and noticed that the burrs had lots of thin strands with hooks at the end of them that attached to loops in the fabric of his clothes. That gave him the idea to use that same method to create his new invention. Velcro makes things stick together by using two sides: one with tiny hooks and the other with tiny loops. Today, it's used on clothes, shoes, backpacks, and many other items. It all started because he was observant.

As you've been reading this book, have you noticed 💡 this on some of the pages? That makes you OBSERVANT!

How many 💡 can you find in the whole book? ....

Now that you know you are observant, you can sharpen your skill and become even better at it. Look around your bedroom or classroom and then have someone take five items out of the room. See if you can identify what was removed.

Curious

When people are curious, what do they do? They ask questions.
A question is a very powerful thing.
Every innovation and discovery started with one person asking
a good question because they were curious.

Why? Good question!
Because questions make you and other people think.
Questions get people talking.
Questions lead to new ideas, which lead to answers or even more questions.

When you are curious and ask questions,
you probably start searching for answers.
That's a big step toward doing something
that could lead to a discovery or invention.

Open-Minded and Creative

People learn new things, have new ideas, and create and invent
when they have their eyes and minds wide open.

There are usually many ways to do something—not just one.
When you are open-minded, you can stretch your imagination
to find solutions that are new, better, or different.

Pretend you are asked to get across a football field in 100 different ways.
You can walk or ride a bike or even do cartwheels. Write down five other
ways you can think of to get from one end zone to the other.

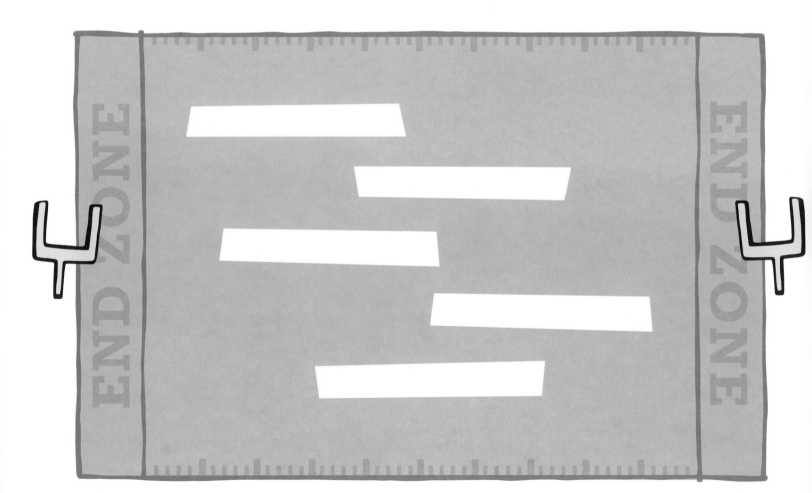

Depending on what you are trying to accomplish,
certain solutions will be better than others.

Now, get even more creative and fill in your ideas below.
You are asked again to cross the field; this time, use your
imagination and fill in the way you could cross the field that is:

The fastest ....

The funniest ....

The cheapest ....

The most expensive ....

The way that uses a partner ....

The most difficult ....

The most time-consuming ....

The way that is not even invented yet...
...except in your mind ....

You just used one of the best practices that inventors use to help them
be open-minded and creative. It's called a brainstorming session. You
started with the problem you wanted to solve (getting across the field)
and came up with a long list of different ways to solve it. For a
brainstorming session, it's good to know that no idea is a bad idea.
That's because most of the time, people find that wild ideas make
them think of unusual solutions that may lead them to their best idea.
You can brainstorm alone or, even better, with a group.

Collaborative

Collaborative means working with other people to accomplish something.

People who innovate, discover, and invent often look back and build on the ideas of others who came before them. For example, the people who invented bikes, cars, and gears could not have invented them if the wheel had not already been invented thousands of years before. People also use past inventions as a starting point to make new ones that are better in some way. Sneakers have been around for a long time, but people keep improving on them by inventing new designs and materials that make them more stylish, more comfortable, or better for a particular sport.

Another way to collaborate is to work together with other people. Usually two minds are better than one. Often hundreds of minds contribute to new discoveries or inventions. That's because people think in different ways and have different skills and talents they can add to the team.

Imagine you are on a soccer team. Do you think it would be fun or successful if you were the only player? Now imagine that everyone on the team was really good at being the goalie. That wouldn't work very well, either. A soccer team works best if some people are fast, others are good at kicking or aiming the ball, and others are good at guarding.

So you see, different skills coming together make a good team.

Collaboration also requires people to work well as a group.

A good team is made up of people who communicate, listen, and support one another.

YOU FIT ON A TEAM

A team is made up of people with different skills who come together to accomplish something.

From the list below, circle the activity that you enjoy the most:

 Writing   Drawing   Reading

 Talking to people   Working with numbers   Playing video games

A team that would be great at creating a video game might include these members:

Designer: This person writes the plan that the team follows to create something fun to play.

Project leader: Groups work best when someone organizes the team members and helps everyone work together by keeping them informed and on schedule.

Artist: To create something new, people often start with a sketch or diagram to help them picture the idea. The artist helps the team see the vision of what they will create.

Programmer: To turn the ideas into a game, this person writes computer code or uses math to tell the computer what to do so someone can play the game.

Researcher: This person spends time looking for information in books, online, and out in the world to help the team make informed decisions.

Tester: Once the game is created, this person plays it to make sure it works as planned by the designer.

Other kinds of inventions and discoveries need team members with different kinds of skills. Are you good at building things? Noticing nature? Keeping a diary? Cheering people on? Speaking to groups? Listening and giving advice?

No matter what skills you have, there is a team that would be right for you!

Systematic

Systematic means something is done in an organized way so one step leads to the next step. For example, if you follow the same routine most mornings as a way to stay organized and get things done, then you're being systematic.

When people want to learn or create new things, they often use proven—systematic—methods to help them. One useful process is called the scientific method. That may sound hard, but it's really just a few easy steps that help people stay organized in order to find answers to questions they have about the world around them.

Ask a question
It all starts with an observation or question. What are you curious about, or what have you seen that makes you wonder?

Do research
In this step, you gather information so you can learn what is already known about your question and topic.

Create a Hypothesis
Here, you make a good guess. What do you think is the answer to your question? That's your hypothesis.

Experiment
Next, you experiment by testing your hypothesis. When you do this, you make careful observations and write down your steps.

Analyze the data
You can look at all the information (the data) you learned to see what it tells you.

Hypothesis is true: You've just proved it.

Hypothesis is false: That's OK. Try again.

Share your findings
Share what you've learned with others and spread the information.

A similar process is called the invention and design method. This systematic process is a series of steps through which anything can be designed, invented, or innovated!

Courageous

People show courage in many different ways.

If someone is afraid to try something new but does it anyway, that's courage. When people stand up for their ideas and beliefs even though others may not agree with them, that's courage. When someone knows that they might not have all the answers but still explores and works to find them, that's courage, too.

Katherine Johnson is a brilliant African American scientist and mathematician who worked at NASA beginning in the 1950s. Her work helped get the first American into space, the first astronaut to orbit Earth, and the Apollo 11 flight to the moon. Throughout her career, she was brave and didn't let barriers stop her. It wasn't common when she was young for girls to get math degrees, but that didn't keep her from following her interests. Her graduate school had been for only white students until she was among the first black students allowed in. She also became the first woman to join an all-male research team working on the space program. Katherine says that she loves to learn and that even when people tried to ignore her, her hand stayed up, she asked questions, and she kept on working to achieve her goals.

The Wright brothers were bicycle makers and dreamers. They were convinced that they could create a machine that flew. Most people at the time didn't think it was possible. The brothers tried many different ways to build a flying machine. The first ones didn't work, but the Wrights kept learning how to improve their designs. They finally succeeded and invented, built, and flew the first airplane. Their success only came after hundreds of flights in gliders, endless work on propeller design, and countless crashes and minor injuries. They were brave to keep trying despite people saying it was impossible.

There are many other examples of courageous people who discovered or created amazing things.

Perseverant

Can you think of a time when something was hard for you to do but you stuck with it, worked through the challenges, and tried your best? Well, that's what it means to be perseverant.

You are probably perseverant every day. When you try to finish homework in your hardest subject instead of giving up; when you are playing a sport and feel really tired but keep going so you won't let your team down; when you are learning a new instrument and practice music over and over again until it sounds right...that's being perseverant.

Part of the process of making anything happen is to try, sometimes make mistakes or face difficulties, and then try and try again!

Here's what two famous inventors and one great athlete said:

"Anyone who has never made a mistake has never tried anything new."
Albert Einstein

"I've missed more than 9,000 shots in my career. I've lost almost 300 games. I've failed over and over and over in my life, and that is why I succeed."
Michael Jordon

"I have not failed. I've just found 10,000 ways that won't work."
Thomas Edison

Many of the best inventors are people who try, mess up, fail, and try again. They are not afraid of getting something wrong. They realize that while they are hoping to accomplish their goal, the process of experimenting helps them learn. Sometimes the process leads to new ideas. Sometimes it leads to new inventions. Sometimes it simply helps them learn what does not work...which is a great thing to know. But no matter what, they understand that they need to be perseverant and push through the hard stuff if they want to reach their goals.

Turn the page to practice being perseverant.

Practice trying and failing...and learning along the way!

START Sometimes it's hard to know which way to go. That's okay; you can try them all if you want.

A Here, you are told a secret word: **mission**. How does this help? Sometimes we learn something and have no idea it's important. It's only later we find out it's helpful to know.

B Ever feel like you're going around in circles? Experimenting and trying to understand how to make something work can sometimes feel that way. That's okay; don't give up.

D Your key to success is a secret word. Do you know it? It has seven letters: M _ _ S _ _ _ .

If you don't know the code, you'll need to go back to the start and try to find it. Sometimes we're really close to our goal but have more work to do before we're done.

If you know the code, write it here:

_____

and cross the finish line.

FINISH You made it! **Congratulations.** You've been wise, patient, and perseverant!

C Yay—you failed! But did you learn something at this stop? On your path to a goal, you sometimes find out that you have part of the answer but not all of it. Here you learn that you should have gone straight at the last corner.

Think about an invention or discovery as if it is a plant or flower. It starts with an idea from your imagination—the seed—but then it needs to be nurtured to make it grow.

When you use your skills of being...

couragious

systematic

curious

creative

perserverant

observant

collaborative

you are giving your idea water and sun, and helping it grow into an amazing thing!

Now that you know that inventors
and scientists are regular people
JUST LIKE YOU...
...it's your turn.

What will you create and discover? How will you change the world?

One way to start thinking about it is to explore the wishes and dreams
you have for yourself, for others, and for the world around you.

Maybe you want to find answers to questions about animals, stars, rocks, people, or other things.

Maybe you want to help people who are sick.

Maybe you wish the world were cleaner and less polluted.

Maybe you care about creating justice and peace in the world.

Maybe you want to build a new business with the next big product.

Maybe you hope to help people who can't see or walk or have other special needs.

Maybe you want to spread fun and entertainment through games, movies, or parks.

Your Wish List

List some things you think would make the world a better place,
or things you wish that you and everyone in the world could have.

....

....

....

....

Just like all of the inventors who came before you,
you have the power to create things to make these wishes come true!

What Activities Do You Enjoy?

Another way to start thinking about what you might create is to think about how
you like to spend your time. Make a list of some of your favorite activities.

....

....

....

....

You may decide to invent things that relate to the items on this list.

Whether they are big or small, all innovations start with
someone trying to solve a problem and then creating a solution.

Make Life Easier

Robots are machines that do things for humans.
People are making robots that can do all sorts of new and cool things.

Some robots do things that are helpful to people—for example, there are robots that can make lunch, clean floors, and check in guests at a hotel. Other robots are built to be fun and entertaining. Robots can sing, play soccer, or even make you smile by dancing or playing your favorite song. Robots are also made to help people do certain jobs. There are robots that help build cars, perform microscopic surgery, and print 3-D objects. Robots can even do things that are sometimes too dangerous for humans to do—like go to Mars or help save someone from a burning building.

Invent a robot that can do anything you can imagine.

Here, you can draw a picture and explain what your robot will do.

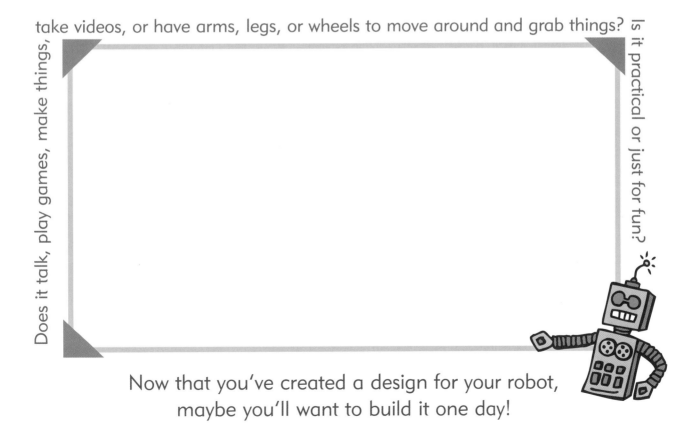

take videos, or have arms, legs, or wheels to move around and grab things?

Is it practical or just for fun?

Does it talk, play games, make things,

Now that you've created a design for your robot,
maybe you'll want to build it one day!

Create a "Bother List"

There are problems and puzzles to solve everywhere.

One way to consider what you may want to invent or create is to think of the things that "bother" you or those around you. People often come up with their best ideas for inventions when they are thinking about things that bother them.

Does it bother you…to walk the dog when it's cold outside? That you can't reach the top shelf of the freezer to get the ice cream? That you have to make your bed? That people get sick? That your grandparents don't understand texting?

Grab a friend, and go on a "bother-me adventure."

Look around your house, school, or community and make a list of the things you notice that bother you or could be done better. Your list can include things that are really big and affect lots of people—like global warming—or things that are smaller and only affect you—like if your backpack is too heavy to carry.

Be a Problem-Solver! Find the Opportunity

As you know, inventors make things to solve problems. To an inventor, things that others may see as a problem really look like an opportunity for something that's waiting to be solved.

Pick three things from your bother list and write down ideas for how you can solve these issues. Your inventions can be ideas that you think can actually be created. But be sure to stretch your imagination with one idea that doesn't exist yet. * For this last one, think of the wildest and craziest way to solve the problem.

Here's an example to get you thinking.

Problem: When it's cold out, it bothers me to walk the dog.

Solutions:
1. Build a fence in the yard so the dog can go outside by itself.
2. Create a heated indoor dog park.
* 3. Train the dog to walk and clean up after itself.

Problem: ....
....

Solutions: ....
1. ....
2. ....
* 3. ....

Problem: ....
....

Solutions: ....
1. ....
2. ....
* 3. ....

Problem: ....
....

Solutions: ....
1. ....
2. ....
* 3. ....

Maybe you'll decide to make one of these solutions into an invention.

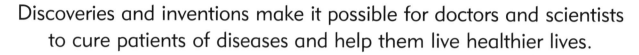

Create a Healthier World

Discoveries and inventions make it possible for doctors and scientists to cure patients of diseases and help them live healthier lives.

Have you ever had a cold?

Did you know that no one has found a way to cure the common cold yet?

This is a health problem that affects almost everyone.

Maybe YOU want to find the cure!

Imagine no runny noses, no sore throats, no sick days in bed.

Here, list any health problems that you hope to cure one day.
You can also write down why these issues are important to you.

....

....

....

....

....

Caring About Clean Water

People need water to live. To stay healthy, we need clean water to drink and to keep basic things around us clean. We also use water every day for things like showers, washing clothes, flushing toilets, and much more.

The fresh water we drink comes from rivers, lakes, and streams. It also comes from underground.

Water that is dirty or polluted can harm the people and animals drinking it. It can also damage plants and even kill animals that live in it.

Some water facts:

- 70% of people in the world don't have clean water to drink.

- Almost 99% of the world's water is undrinkable because it is salty or frozen in ice caps. That means that just 1% of all the water on earth is healthy for people to drink.

What can we do? Good question!

New ideas and technologies are being developed to find ways to provide clean water to everyone.

Ask an adult to do some research with you. See what you can learn about some of these ideas: desalination, recycling water, purifying water with chemical tablets, rainwater catchment systems, using ultraviolet light to purify water.

Maybe you want to join the teams of inventors that are working to create new ways to help people and protect our planet so we can have enough clean water for everyone.

Smart Clothes

You've probably heard of a smartphone, but have you heard of a smart car or a smart house? These things are "smart" because they have technology inside them that allows them to do cool things that help people. For example, a smart refrigerator might know when your family is out of milk and send your parent a text reminder to buy more.

Maybe you want to get in on this trend by creating smart clothes for the future.

Will your shirt be able to change its color or design based on your mood?
Will you be able to ask your pants for directions so you never get lost?
Will you create a coat that makes you invisible? Maybe your clothes will wash themselves when they're dirty, or get larger as you grow.

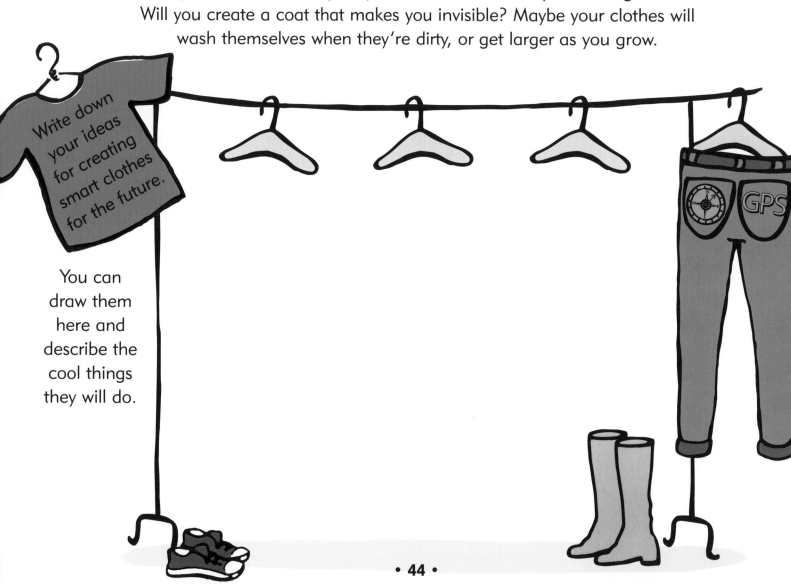

Write down your ideas for creating smart clothes for the future.

You can draw them here and describe the cool things they will do.

GPS

Super Senses

People use their senses to experience the world.
The five common ones are seeing, hearing, smelling, tasting, and touching.

Pick one of your senses and describe an invention that you
would like to create to make it stronger, better, or supersensitive.
This could be used in the future to help people who lost that sense,
or it could be used to give everyone superhuman abilities.

What would you create and why?

Invent a New Recipe

By experimenting with different ingredients and ways to mix and match them, people have created treats you may enjoy all the time like soda, bubblegum, or Popsicles. Sometimes people combine their favorite things and end up creating something delicious. Someone who liked ice cream and cookies probably invented the ice-cream sandwich that way!

Menu

What is your favorite snack food?

What are some ingredients that you like?

Ingredients

Can you come up with a new recipe that includes your favorite tastes?

It's Fun to Invent 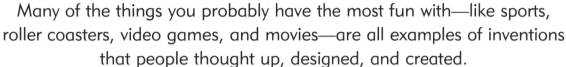!

Many of the things you probably have the most fun with—like sports, roller coasters, video games, and movies—are all examples of inventions that people thought up, designed, and created.

Why not join these fun-creators and invent a new game?

Here are some questions to get you thinking about your new game: Does your game use a ball—like soccer—or does it use cards, tokens, or other objects in order to play? Is it played on a board, in a field, on the computer, or somewhere else? What are the instructions and rules? What is the goal of the game, and how do you win? What will you name your game?

You can design your game on your own or ask your family or friends to join in and help. Describe your game here:

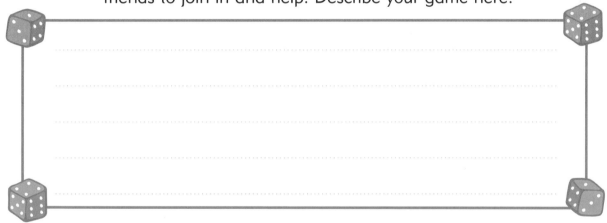

Now that you've invented a new game, ask some friends to play it with you. This will let you test your game. Next, ask yourself and whoever played with you some questions: Did the game work? Was it fun? Are there other ideas that can make it even better? You can go back and improve your game based on these answers.

You just used your imagination to form a new idea. You created it. You tested it. You collaborated. You improved it. Your game is ready to be shared with the world. YOU are an inventor!

Break the Code

What would you do if you wanted to give information to someone but also keep your message private? Use a code!

Cryptography uses puzzles, logic, or math to invent secret languages that people can use to pass along messages.

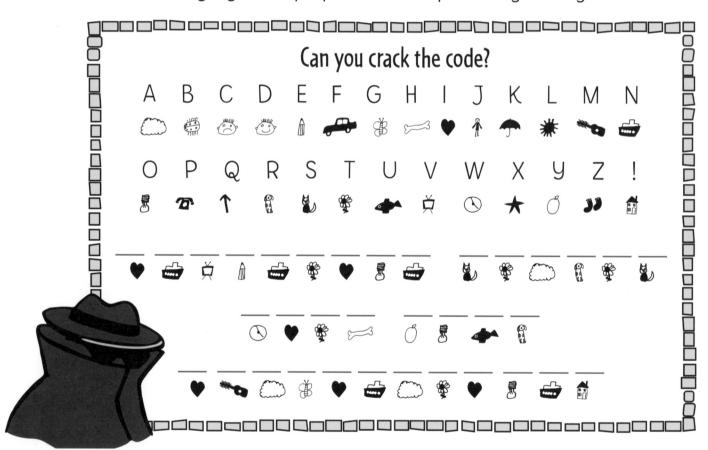

Can you crack the code?

Did you figure it out?   Here's the message: ¡uoᴉʇɐuᴉƃɐɯᴉ ɹnoʎ ɥʇᴉʍ sʇɹɐʇs uoᴉʇuǝʌuI

Here's another way to share a private message:

Using science, you can communicate a secret message with invisible ink.
Here's how: Dip a cotton swab in lemon juice and use it to write a message on a piece of paper. Later, when you're ready to reveal the note, dry the paper with a hair dryer. Since you must be curious, you can do research to learn why the heat caused the ink to show up.

Predict the Future

In fairy tales, fortune-tellers can look into the future and predict what is going to happen.

In real life, there are actually people who work to predict the future. They use their math and computer skills to look at lots of tiny bits of information from the past (called data) to figure out what is likely to happen in the future.

People who do this apply their skills in many different ways. For example, they can:

- Try to figure out when and where there will be a hurricane or storm so they can warn people in advance and help keep them safe.

- Predict the kinds of songs you may like based on the music you've listened to in the past and even send you suggestions for a great playlist that's perfect for your taste.

- Help a sports team. A coach could look at information and know which baseball player would be best to hire.

- Help doctors predict how to best keep you and others healthy based on information about a family's history.

- Design roads or adjust stoplights in ways that reduce traffic during busy hours to help create smart cities.

If you could see into the future, what would you want to know?

Just think…if you put your mind to it and learn the skills, you too can become a fortune-teller!

Just Build It!

Using your imagination, planning, and other skills are key to creating something, but sometimes you'll have the most fun when you get to jump in and build something.

Here are some fun things you can try making.

Put a check ✓ next to the projects you want to do, and then get building!

- Want to measure the wind? Build an anemometer, and you'll have a device to tell you the speed of the wind each day

- Build the tallest structure you can, using only things found in nature

- Make a cloaking device with mirrors and see how you can make something seem to disappear

- Create a mini roller coaster using marbles and foam tubing

- Create a musical greeting card and send it to a friend or family member

- Build a fort, game, or other structure using cardboard

- Build a baking-soda volcano and watch it erupt

- Make a homemade musical instrument

- Build a clock using potatoes

Ask an adult for help in finding supplies, materials, and online tips to tackle these projects. Together, you can search websites for "how to build a (fill-in-the-word)," and you'll find ideas that can get you started. Then, of course, you can use your imagination to try new things that will make your creations unique and different.

Take a picture of your favorite creations and glue or tape them here.

For the last project, find an object in your house
and take it apart with an adult. (It can be an old clock, chair,
radio, bicycle…pretty much anything not being used anymore.)

Take a picture of all the
pieces and put that here.

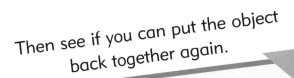

Then see if you can put the object
back together again.

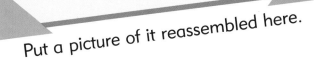

Put a picture of it reassembled here.

Take STEPS to Become a Lifelong Creator

Wow! You have what it takes to be a lifelong creator!

And if you don't believe me, you can be scientific; just look back through your book and you will find a lot of data and evidence that proves it!

You have a great imagination.

You have lots of ideas.

You have the qualities of an inventor and scientist.

You notice problems that are waiting to be solved.

You create solutions.

You also know that it takes hard work and action to turn your ideas into reality.

So now think about some steps you can take that will help you on your journey to creating a future full of your creations.

Goals and Planning

A goal is something that you want to achieve.

If you love being creative, helping the world, and inventing things, and you want to do it even more, then that's a goal.

When you have a goal, there are always steps you need to take to make it happen. It takes work and planning. The things you do today and tomorrow will help you accomplish your goals in the future.

☑ **Learn:** The more you study and learn about science, technology, engineering, math, art, and design, the more opportunities you will have to turn your ideas into real-life solutions.

☑ **Experiment:** A great way to learn is to jump in and do it . . . and do it . . . and do it some more.

☑ **Find fun places to practice and play:** There are tons of camps, contests, parks and programs all over the country that offer fun ways to use your imagination and create things. Ask an adult to help you find opportunities near you.

Create Something TODAY

There's no time like the present to take a step, imagine, and create.
The more you do it, the more fun you will have.

I, _____ , will invent or create _____
(your name)   (give it a name)

because _____.
(describe the problem it will solve or its purpose)

Here, you can write down your idea or draw a picture of something you would like to create. It can be a story, a business, a machine, a new medicine, or anything else that your awesome imagination can dream up!

Group Activities

If one person can imagine and create many things,
a group of people can do even more!

Here are just a few fun ways for you and your friends to share the magic of discovery, creation, and invention.

⭐ Take your friends to a science museum and see what there is to discover.

⭐ Have all of your IMAGINE IT BOOK friends form an Inventors Club, where you can get together to share and improve your inventions.

⭐ Build something. Find some materials from around your house. Then have a 30-minute challenge to build something with friends and family.

⭐ Host a brainstorming party where guests pick an object and come up with as many different ways as possible to make it better.

⭐ Visit a "Makerspace" in your community. There, you will find tools and gadgets and get to meet great people who are tinkering, fixing, inventing, building, and having fun!

⭐ Invite an expert to your classroom or group to share ideas and talk about their work. This person could be a video-game developer, a scientist, a builder, an engineer, or anyone else who gets to spend their time inventing.

Wear Your Imagination Proudly

Some people may forget how cool invention and discovery are.
You can remind them through your art.

Make a T-shirt that celebrates imagination.

What else can you write on your T-shirts?

You can also share your message through art by making posters, writing poems, taking pictures, or creating songs.

Search for Mentors

A mentor is a person who has skills, advice, or experience that they are
willing to share with another person to help inspire them.
Mentors can help you on your journey to becoming an inventor or scientist.

If you want a mentor, where can you find one?

The first step is to think about the kinds of things you hope to learn, practice, or do.
I am interested in...........................and...................................... .

A mentor can be someone you know—like a parent, teacher, or coach. Some people
I know who are good at the things on my list are.....................and...................... .
A mentor can also be someone you've never met before who is really good at something
and willing to help you learn about it.

People who are good at the things on my list may work at these kinds of places or jobs:
.... Some people I'd love to meet who inspire me
are..................................and...................................... .

Here, you can write a note to someone you think would be a good mentor for you.

Tell that person
why you admire
them and what
you hope to
learn from them.

You can write
to someone
you know or to
someone you've
never met—like
a famous thinker,
leader, or inventor.

Interview Someone Amazing

There are many people around you with jobs that let them imagine, discover, create, and invent. They are doctors, architects, mathematicians, engineers, artists, and many others.
Ask a parent to help you find someone in your community to talk to.
Grab a pencil, imagine you are a reporter, and write down the answers you discover.

The News

SUNDAY, MARCH 26

VOL. III, NUMBER IV

What made you choose your profession?

....

....

What do you like best about it?

....

....

....

What are your favorite inventions from history?

....

....

....

What are you working on now?

....

....

....

....

....

What advice do you have for me?

....

....

....

....

....

....

OTHER STUFF

YAY YOU!

Congratulations!

This IMAGINE IT BOOK certificate shows that you have what it takes to shape the world with your imagination.

THE IMAGINE IT BOOK
This certificate is awarded to

....
WRITE YOUR NAME HERE

for using your imagination to discover, create, and invent new ideas and new things.

....
DATE

Now that you know how great it feels to nurture your ideas, get out there and keep it up: Tackle new problems, find new answers, and learn as much as you can so you can bring your creations to life.

OTHER STUFF

Join Watering Can® Press in growing kids with character.

www.wateringcanpress.com

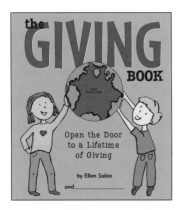
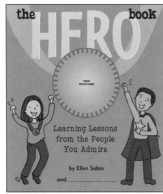
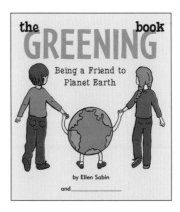
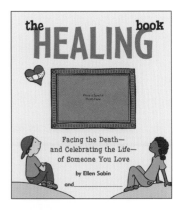

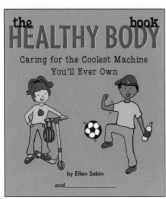
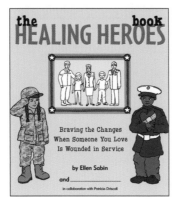
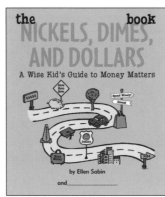
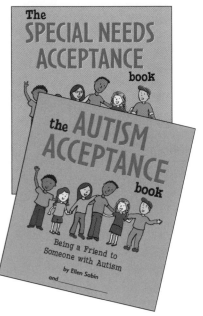

- Find and order other Watering Can® books.
- Take advantage of bulk discounts for schools and organizations.
- Learn about customizing our books for corporate and community outreach.
- View the FREE Teacher's Guides and Parent's Guides available on our site.

We hope you always remember
the amazing things you can do
when you use your imagination
and nurture your ideas!